Baby Animals
Learn and Play

First published by Experience Early Learning Company
7243 Scotchwood Lane, Grawn, Michigan 49637 USA

Text Copyright ©2013 by Experience Early Learning Co.
Printed and bound in the USA

ISBN: 978-1-937954-10-9
Visit us at www.ExperienceEarlyLearning.com

Baby Animals Learn and Play

experience™
Early Learning

Bear cubs climb up rocks.

What can you climb?

A baby turtle
crawls quickly to the sea.

How fast can you
cr a w l?

A baby orangutan swings in a tree.

Where do you swing?

A baby opossum likes
to hang with his tail.

What part of your body
helps you hang?

A baby fox hides
in the grass.

Where can you
hide?

A baby gorilla rides
on his mommy's back.

Who
carries
you?

An elephant calf
drinks with his trunk.

What do you use
to take a drink?

A baby leopard
learns to catch a treat.

What can you catch?

A baby penguin
snuggles with his dad.

Who do you
snuggle?

A fawn takes a rest
at the end of the day.

When do you rest?

Baby animals learn and play.
Which of these actions can you do today?

crawl

catch

climb

swing

hide

hang

drink

ride

snuggle

and then take a rest... zzzzzzZZZZ

Experience Early Learning specializes in the development and publishing of research-based curriculum, books, music and authentic assessment tools for early childhood teachers and parents around the world. Our mission is to inspire children to experience learning through creative expression, play and open-ended discovery. We believe educational materials that invite children to participate with their whole self (mind, body and spirit) support on-going development and encourage children to become the authors of their own unique learning stories.

www.ExperienceEarlyLearning.com